D0792272

Produced by AA Publishing
Captions by Richard Cavendish

Filmset by Wyvern Typesetting Ltd, Bristol
Colour separation by Fotographics Ltd
Printed and bound in China, produced by Mandarin Offset

The contents of this publication are believed correct
at the time of printing. Nevertheless, the publishers
cannot accept responsibility for errors or omissions,
or for changes in details given.

© The Automobile Association 1992

All rights reserved. No part of this publication may
be reproduced, stored in a retrieval system, or
transmitted in any form or by any means –
electronic, photocopying, recording or otherwise –
unless the written permission of the publishers has
been obtained beforehand.

A CIP catalogue record for this book is available
from the British Library.

Published by The Automobile Association, Fanum
House, Basing View, Basingstoke, Hampshire
RG21 2EA.

ISBN 0 7495 0392 0

Front cover: Top – *View from Gillbrow*
Main – *Skiddaw, from Cat Bells*
Back cover: *Reflections in Buttermere*
Title page (opposite): *Fell walkers above Grasmere*

LAKE DISTRICT

Visions of the Lake District captures the breathtaking beauty of this most spectacular region of Britain in a range of the finest images from the AA's picture library. Charming villages, remote farms, soaring fells and crystal-clear lakes form the romantic backdrop for the Lakeland people and their crafts — small wonder this is Britain's most visited area.

Below *Gorse in blazing flower near Buttermere, deep in the heart of the Lake District and widely regarded as the prettiest of its valleys. The scenery of this region of Cumbria was carved and shaped aeons ago by ice, as giant glaciers gouged out the landscape.*

Above *Pastoral beauty on the way to Buttermere from Portiscale. People followed the ice in moulding the landscape of the Lake District, and one of its delights is the contrast between the high, rugged fells above and the enclosed, gentle farming country below.*

Left *Boats drawn up at the lakeside near Crag Wood, on Buttermere. The lake is owned and protected by the National Trust, and the circular walk round its shore is particularly enjoyable.*

Following spread *Where the road between Keswick and Cockermouth passes through Buttermere. The beauty of the Lake District was first discovered by the outside world in the 18th century, when a new interest in wild and picturesque mountain scenery was born.*

Left *According to treasured family tradition, the glass bowl known as 'the Luck of Muncaster' was given to the Penningtons of Muncaster Castle by King Henry VI in the 15th century, for sheltering him from his enemies.*

Below *Built in the 14th century, and enlarged and embellished by Anthony Salvin in the 1860s and 1870s, Muncaster Castle is famous for its rhododendron gardens and its incomparable views of the Esk Valley and the Lake District fells.*

Opposite page *Mellowed by time, the ruins of Brougham Castle stand guard by the River Eamont. This medieval stronghold near Penrith was built to command the point where the main road to Scotland crossed the route from York. The Romans had chosen the same site for a fort centuries earlier.*

11

Above *Many of the castles which once guarded the Lake District have crumbled into decay with the years. Katherine Parr, the last of Henry VIII's six wives, was born at Kendal Castle, whose ruins stand high above the old market town.*

Right *Near Kendal is Sizergh Castle, for centuries home of the Strickland family and now owned by the National Trust. The core of the house is a medieval pele tower, into which everyone in the area could retreat when danger threatened.*

Left *Penrith Castle was one of a chain of strongholds guarding the strategic route along the Eden Valley into and out of Scotland. It was rebuilt by one of the Stricklands in the 14th century, at a time when Penrith was often attacked by Scots raiders.*

Following spread *Coniston Farm is a typical Lakeland farmhouse, with its barn and outbuildings set against a backdrop of rolling fells. The durable local granite and slate were used to build walls and roofs, and the walls were limewashed against damp.*

Left *This farm is sheltered below the fells near Thelkeld. Far back in the Stone Age, farmers cleared the Lakeland forests, and sheep have been the mainstay of agriculture on the poor soil of the Lake District for centuries past.*

Above *Herdwick sheep at the Eskdale Show. Herdwicks are the local breed, small and hardy, tough enough to withstand the fierce winters on the fells. They grow up on their home hillside and rarely ever stray from it. All Herdwick lambs are born black, and their fleeces whiten with age.*

Left *A shepherd and his dog keep an eye on their flock above Longsleddale, the narrow valley of the River Sprint. Well within living memory shepherds in the region used an archaic dialect, said to be of Celtic origin, for counting sheep. This may date back to a time when the Anglo-Saxon settlers employed native British shepherds.*

Right *The Lake District was never as wealthy an area as the more fertile lowlands of England, but the local gentry built themselves some fine houses nevertheless. This clock tower crowns the stables at Holker Hall.*

Right *At Graythwaite Hall, near Far Sawrey and close to the west bank of Windermere, the 19th-century gardens are open to visitors. The house is one of the few examples of an unfortified mansion built before 1600 in this area. It was remodelled in the 1880s.*

Right *At Troutbeck, to the north-east of Windermere, Townend House was built in the 17th century for one of the well-to-do farming families who were known as 'statesmen'. The house was never modernised and still contains the handsome furniture and rich wooden panelling originally designed for it. Today it belongs to the National Trust.*

Below *Holker Hall dates back to the 16th century, but was partly rebuilt for the Cavendish family after a bad fire in the 1870s. The gardens were laid out by the great Joseph Paxton, the designer of the Crystal Palace in London.*

Right *One of the old lead drainpipes at Levens Hall. This Elizabethan house, south of Kendal, is one of the showplaces of the Lake District, with fine furniture, panelling and plasterwork.*

Below *The famous topiary garden of box and yew at Levens Hall was laid out in 1692 by a Frenchman named Beaumont who also planted the beech hedge, now 20ft (6m) tall, and the avenue of limes. The house also has a handsome deer park.*

Left *Thousands of flowers and much hard work bring the gardens of Levens Hall to brilliant life in spring and summer. The garden has a resident ghost, 'the Grey Lady' — but if she fails to materialise, there are working model steam engines to fall back on.*

Below *Levens Hall, seen from the gardens. The site was originally occupied by a medieval pele tower, built for defence against marauding Scots. In more peaceful times a comfortable Elizabethan mansion was added by the Bellingham family, who made a fortune out of the dissolution of the monasteries and later gambled it away.*

Lake District

Right *Bust of William Wordsworth at Cockermouth, the town where he was born. The great poet spent most of his life in the Lake District. The area inspired much of his poetry, which in turn has drawn generations of visitors to explore the countryside that he loved.*

Above *Dove Cottage at Grasmere was the home of Wordsworth, his wife Mary and his sister Dorothy until 1808, and much of his best work was written there, including the 'Ode on Intimations of Immortality' and* The Prelude. *The diminutive cottage is today preserved as a literary shrine.*

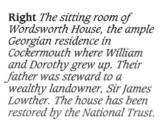

Right *The sitting room of Wordsworth House, the ample Georgian residence in Cockermouth where William and Dorothy grew up. Their father was steward to a wealthy landowner, Sir James Lowther. The house has been restored by the National Trust.*

Above *A host of golden daffodils dancing in the breeze at Ullswater inspired a famous poem. Wordsworth was a formidable walker, who covered miles over fell and dale with a devouring stride and responded passionately to the Lakeland countryside.*

Left *Daffodils in Dora's Field at Rydal Mount, where the Wordsworths spent their last years. Dora was the poet's much-loved daughter, who tyrannised lovingly over him. He never recovered from the blow of her death in 1847.*

Following spread *View across Grasmere to the village. Wordsworth called this 'the loveliest spot that man hath ever found'. He and his wife, Dorothy and Dora all lie buried in the quiet village churchyard.*

Above *A rowing boat waits patiently at the island in Grasmere. One of the peculiarities of the Lakes is that the word 'lake' is so seldom used. With the solitary exception of Bassenthwaite Lake, the lakes are all named 'waters', 'meres' or 'tarns'.*

Left *Enjoying the scene at Grasmere. Everything in view is part of the Lake District National Park, which was set up in 1951 to preserve this special corner of England. Wordsworth himself had paved the way for this development by describing the Lakes as 'a sort of national property, in which every man has a right and interest who has an eye to perceive and a heart to enjoy'.*

Below *Ready for the off at a hound trail at Loweswater. The course of ten miles is laid by dragging a rag soaked in paraffin and aniseed over it. It takes 20 minutes or so for the fastest dogs to reappear, to a tremendous hubbub of encouraging shouts, whistles and rattled cans from their owners and backers.*

28

Right *Wrestling has been a popular country sport in Britain since at least Roman times. The Cumberland and Westmorland local style is particularly stately and dignified. The wrestlers wear white singlets and tights, often with vividly coloured trunks.*

Left *Judging an array of shepherd's crooks at 'Dog Day' in Patterdale, a small village close to Ullswater. Wool was spun at home on the farm in the old days and taken for sale to market towns like Kendal and Hawkshead.*

Following spread *A view of the fells near Hayeswater in the eastern part of the Lake District, in what was once a lead-mining area. The Lakeland landscape knows every mood, from the benign and serene to the dour, the grim and the positively vicious.*

29

Left *Coaxing them into the pen: sheepdog trials at Patterdale. With the mechanisation of Lakeland farming, the arts of the shepherd have become both a tourist attraction and a valued opportunity to demonstrate skill and individuality.*

Lake District

Above *The venerable steamer Tern, built in 1891, still plies a route on Windermere. There are regular services up and down the lake connecting with the Lakeside and Haverthwaite Railway. The lake itself is England's largest, and is crowded with cruise vessels, yachts and motor boats.*

Left *These smart Victorian pleasure-craft are sedately penned in the Windermere Steamboat Museum, on the eastern side of the lake. Businessmen from Manchester were already building themselves villas on the Windermere lakeshore in Wordsworth's day, and in 1847 the arrival of the railway opened the gates to a tidal wave of visitors.*

Above *Another veteran is the steamer* Lady of the Lake, *which takes an hour or so to traverse the winding 7-mile length of Ullswater, in its beautiful setting below Helvellyn. Ullswater is also a favourite lake for sailing.*

Left *Under gentle oar power on Grasmere, seen from the island in the lake. Among its many other pleasures, the Lake District is a good place for 'messing about in boats', and Arthur Ransome set his 'Swallows and Amazons' books for children here.*

Following spread *Sailboats lie calmly at anchor on gently rippling Derwentwater, the island-studded 'Queen of the Lakes'. There are circular boat trips from Keswick as well as pleasant walks among the wooded crags on both the western and the eastern shores. Much of the land here belongs to the National Trust.*

35

Right *'A perfect combination of the Venetian Gondola and the English Steam Yacht', as she was described when she was launched in 1859, the 'Gondola' provides the ideal way of enjoying the beauty of Coniston Water. With a serpent at her prow (above) and operated by the National Trust, she gives a safer ride than Bluebird, in which Sir Malcolm Campbell set a new world waterspeed record here in 1939. Donald Campbell was killed on this lake in 1967.*

Lake District

Left *View over Derwentwater from Friar's Crag. This celebrated viewpoint is owned by the National Trust, which acquired it in 1922 in memory of Canon Hardwicke Rawnsley of Crosthwaite, a redoubtable defender of the Lakes against damaging development, and one of the Trust's founders.*

Right *Looking south across glimmering Derwentwater to the looming Jaws of Borrowdale, which open on to one of the Lake District's most beautiful valleys, below Great Gable and Scafell Pike. Hugh Walpole, who lived in this area, set his best-selling 'Herries' novels here.*

Left *Boat landings near Friar's Crag. Lakeland scenery struck the 18th-century eye with its resemblance to the kind of Arcadian scenes painted by Claude and Poussin. Artists including Gainsborough, Constable and Turner went to the Lake District on painting expeditions, and their work whetted the appetite of visitors for Lakeland scenery.*

Above *The towns and villages of the Lake District are naturally found on the sheltered low ground, in the shadow of the high hills. This is Coniston, which lies between Coniston Water and the peak called the Old Man. John Ruskin, the Victorian art critic and social reformer, lived just outside the town at Brantwood, and is buried in the churchyard.*

Left *Blossoms are reflected in a cottage window at Cartmel, a pleasant village in southern Lakeland which is a centre for artists and craftspeople. It also boasts a racecourse and a fine church.*

Lake District

Right *Ambleside, in the old county of Westmorland, is a popular tourist centre close to Windermere. The little two-room Bridge House, which perches on a bridge over the swirling water of the Stock Ghyll, was built in the 16th century as a summerhouse and apple store for Ambleside House.*

Below *An old-fashioned equipage waits for customers outside a hotel in the centre of Ambleside. The town has a long history, and stands at the crossing point of several old packhorse routes. The town grew rapidly in Victorian times, to cater for the increasing number of tourists.*

Right *A bravado of baskets outside a craft shop in Hawkshead. Traditional crafts are thriving in the Lake District, in response to demand from visitors for souvenirs and presents with genuine local character. Products include pottery, glass, textiles and rugs.*

Following spread *A gentle farming landscape in southern Lakeland near Broughton in Furness, where the River Duddon comes sweetly down from the hills to the Duddon Sands and the sea. Much of the area was dominated in the Middle Ages by Furness Abbey, one of the richest houses in England, whose abbot held sway here like a petty king.*

Left *Traditional food is a Lakeland speciality too, with Grasmere gingerbread and Kendal mint cake. This engagingly old-fashioned bakery shop window is in Hawkshead, the town where Wordsworth went to school and idly cut his initials on a desk which can still be seen.*

Left *Cumberland sausages, like a rope stuffed with coarsely chopped pork, are on offer at a provision shop in Waberthwaite, on the Esk estuary, near the west coast. Herdwick lamb, Rum Nicky, Westmorland Pie and the local cheeses are also guaranteed to make the mouth water.*

43

Below *Churches preserve the memory of centuries of Christianity in the North. This impressive Norman doorway of the church of St Mary and St Bega, at St Bees on the Cumbrian Coast, dates from the mid-12th century. There was a nunnery here long before that, but its church was destroyed by raiding Vikings.*

46

Above *In the 7th century Anglian (English) settlers spread into the British Celtic territory of Cumbria (the name is closely related to the Welsh word for Wales, Cymru). The church at Irton, near the west coast, is Victorian, but in the churchyard behind is a 9th-century carved Anglian cross.*

Left *'D'ye ken John Peel with his coat so grey?' The famous huntsman's grave is in the churchyard at Caldbeck, and the tombstone is decorated with hunting horns. Peel died in 1854. His wife and their children are also buried here.*

Above *The medieval priory church of Cartmel became the parish church after the dissolution of the monasteries, and was restored in 1620 by George Preston of Holker Hall. Curiously, the upper part of the tower is set diagonally on the lower part. Inside are tablets commemorating people who drowned trying to cross the treacherous sands of Morecambe Bay.*

48

Left *Some of the small churches that ministered to tiny congregations among the remote fells were built much like houses or barns. The church at Matterdale, in the hill country to the north of Ullswater, was built in response to a petition of 1566 by the local people.*

Left *A cherub is holding a portrait medallion on the memorial in Cartmel Priory to one of the Lowther family, who lived at nearby Holker Hall in the 18th century. The Lowthers were one of the leading families in the area, and eventually became Earls of Lonsdale.*

Opposite page *The church of St Bride at Bridekirk, near Cockermouth, is noted for its remarkable 12th-century font, decorated with both Christian and Norse motifs and with an inscription in runes. Two dragons can be seen in the top row. Many Vikings settled in the North and Norse influence was strong.*

51

Above *Elterwater is a small village among the fells at the opening of Great Langdale valley, west of Ambleside. The village is seen here from across its open common. The valley leads on to the foot of the towering Langdale Pikes, which are among the most dramatic peaks in the Lake District.*

Left *Tarn Hows, a famous Lakeland beauty spot between Hawkshead and Coniston, is a man-made lake, created in Victorian times. There are fine views of Coniston Water, the Langdale Pikes and Helvellyn to the north. Tarn Hows belongs to the National Trust, Lakeland's largest landowner.*

Left *The great snow-covered bulk of Skiddaw towers in the distance beyond the blue gleam of Derwentwater. The view is from Ashness Bridge, near the hamlet of Watendlath, east of Borrowdale: the setting for Hugh Walpole's novel* Judith Paris.

Below *The Lake District scenery was created by a blend of geology and natural forces with human action. Stone is the basic natural resource and generations of Lakelanders have used it and worked it. These cairns, called the Nine Standards, are set on the high Westmorland fells east of Shap, on the Coast to Coast Walk.*

53

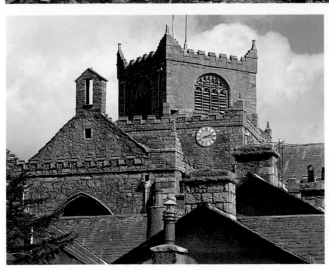

Left *Buildings in the local limestone cluster close to Cartmel's priory church. The odd angle of the upper section of the church tower is particularly evident in this picture: it has been described as 'structurally dubious but visually entertaining'.*

Opposite page *The narrow road snakes its precarious way through the mountain bulwarks of the Honister Pass, between Buttermere and Seatoller, among boulders dropped by the Ice Age glacier which originally carved out this route. Slate has been quarried here since the 17th century.*

Lake District

Opposite page *The central Lake District mountains defeated even the heroic 19th-century railway engineers, and Windermere was the only town in central Lakeland with a station. There were some lines on the periphery, however, and the Lakeside and Haverthwaite Railway runs steam trains on part of the old branch line between Ulverston and the foot of Windermere.*

Right *Like a delightful toy, this Ravenglass and Eskdale train is puffing its way diligently past Muncaster Mill on its route between the coast and scenic Eskdale.*

Above *The Ravenglass and Eskdale, here at Ravenglass station, is a miniature 15-inch gauge railway. The line was originally built in 1875 to carry ore from the iron mines at Nab Gill, seven miles into Eskdale, near Boot. It soon carried passengers as well.*

Right *The locomotive is dwarfed by its handlers. The line would have closed in 1960, but was saved by a private preservation company which bought it and operates it successfully through the summer.*

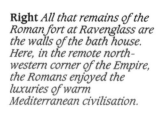

Above *The indomitable Romans drove a road from Ambleside through the Hardknott Pass, one of the highest in the Lake District, to reach the Irish Sea at Ravenglass. They built a stone fort to guard the pass. On a spur 700ft (210m) up, it is now in the care of English Heritage.*

Right *All that remains of the Roman fort at Ravenglass are the walls of the bath house. Here, in the remote north-western corner of the Empire, the Romans enjoyed the luxuries of warm Mediterranean civilisation.*

Below *Bassenthwaite Lake lies submissively below the Skiddaw range. Four miles long and a conservation area, it is one of the biggest of the lakes, the one furthest to the north and the only one which is actually called 'lake'.*

Following spread *Idyllic Esthwaite Water. Wordsworth wrote: 'I do not know any tract of country in which in so narrow a compass may be found an equal variety in the influence of light and shadow . . .'*

Right *Isolated and grim, Wast Water lies beneath its steep dark wall of rock and scree, which rears up almost vertically from the water. This is the deepest lake in England, going down below sea level. It is owned and protected by the National Trust.*

Below *Ennerdale Water, looking towards Pillar Mountain. This is the most westerly, most remote and least frequented of the lakes. It was here that William Wordsworth came to the conclusion that to one born and bred among the Lakes, the thought of death sat easy.*

Above *Crummock Water is yet another beautiful lake, five miles long and guarded by high, impervious fells. It lies close to Buttermere and was once part of it.*

Left *Loweswater's name means 'leafy lake'. Small and attractively secluded, about a mile long, it was originally part of the same large lake as Buttermere and Crummock Water, but is now concealed from them by rocks deposited by a melting glacier. It, too, is owned by the National Trust.*

Index

Acknowledgements

The Automobile Association wishes to thank the following photographers and libraries for their assistance in the preparation of this book.

DEREK FORSS Front Cover Skiddaw from Cat Bells, Back Cover Buttermere Pines

The remaining photographs are from the Automobile Association's own photo library (AA Photo Library) with contributions from:

Malc Birkitt, Ted Bowness, Rick Cizja, Sara King, Peter Sharpe and Richard Surman.